W9-BZO-526

CHESTERFIELD COUNTY PUBLIC LIBRARY
CHESTERFIELD, VA

Amazing Bees

By Sue Unstead

Series Editor Deborah Lock
US Senior Editor Shannon Beatty
Editor Arpita Nath
Senior Art Editor Ann Cannings
Art Editor Yamini Panwar
Producer, Pre-Production Dragana Puvacic
Picture Researcher Aditya Katyal
DTP Designers Syed Md Farhan, Dheeraj Singh
Managing Editor Soma B. Chowdhury
Managing Art Editor Ahlawat Gunjan
Art Director Martin Wilson

Reading Consultant
Linda Gambrell, Ph.D.

First American Edition, 2016
Published in the United States by DK Publishing
345 Hudson Street, New York, New York 10014

Copyright © 2016 Dorling Kindersley Limited.
DK, a Division of Penguin Random House LLC
16 17 18 19 20 10 9 8 7 6 5 4 3 2 1
001-285386-July/16

All rights reserved. Without limiting the rights under copyright reserved above, no part of this publication
may be reproduced, stored in or introduced into a retrieval system, or transmitted, in any form, or by any
means (electronic, mechanical, photocopying, recording, or otherwise), without the prior written permission
of the copyright owner. Published in Great Britain by Dorling Kindersley Limited.

A catalog record for this book is available
from the Library of Congress.

ISBN: 978-1-4654-4604-6 (Paperback)
ISBN: 978-1-4654-4603-9 (Hardback)

DK books are available at special discounts when purchased in bulk for sales promotions,
premiums, fund-raising, or educational use. For details, contact:
DK Publishing Special Markets
345 Hudson Street, New York, New York 10014
SpecialSales@dk.com

Printed and bound in China.

The publisher would like to thank the following for their kind permission to reproduce their photographs:
(Key: a=above, b=below/bottom, c=center, l=left, r=right, t=top)
1 Alamy Images: Kevin Read. **3 123RF.com:** Martin Deja (tr, crb, cb). **4–5 naturepl.com:** Kim Taylor. **6 Dreamstime.com:** Tharvron Posri (t).
Science Photo Library: (b). **7 Corbis:** Lumi Images/Romulic-Stojcic. **8 Dreamstime.com:** Lorrainehudgins (clb); Tomas1111 (cr). **9 123RF.com:** sumikophoto
(cl). **Dreamstime.com:** Brian Maudsley (tr). **10 Corbis:** Visuals Unlimited/Robert Pickett. **11 Alamy Images:** David Wootton (tr).
Dreamstime.com: Angelshot (tc); Petro Perutskyy (c). **12 Dreamstime.com:** Dichapongp (bl); Matthew Heizman (cr). **13 Dreamstime.com:** Juefraphoto (cr).
naturepl.com: John B Free (clb). **14 Dreamstime.com:** Tharvron Posri (t). **14–15 iStockphoto.com:** GomezDavid. **16 Dreamstime.com:** Kavcicm.
17 Dreamstime.com: Valpal. **18 123RF.com:** Burmakin Andrey (cra); Hiroshi Tanaka (b). **19 Science Photo Library:** Cordelia Molloy (clb, br).
20 Alamy Images: Stonemeadow Photography. **21 Dreamstime.com:** Dave Massey. **22 Dreamstime.com:** Serban Enache (c). **24 Dreamstime.com:** Tharvron
Posri. **26–27 Alamy Images:** Nature Picture Library/Kim Taylor. **28 Alamy Images:** D. Hurst. **29 Getty Images:** Copyright OneliaPG Photography.
30–31 Dreamstime.com: Harold Bivens. **32 Dreamstime.com:** Alexandru Razvan Cofaru (clb); Piliphoto (tr); Nitr (bc). **33 Alamy Images:** Nature Picture
Library/Simon Colmer (tl). **Dreamstime.com:** Irochka (cr); Lshtandel (bl). **34 Dreamstime.com:** Tharvron Posri (t). **Getty Images:** Visuals Unlimited, Inc./
Eric Tourneret (b). **35 Corbis:** Minden Pictures/NIS/Agustin Esmoris. **36 Getty Images:** Stavros Markopoulos (bl). **naturepl.com:** PREMAPHOTOS (cra).
37 Alamy Images: Nigel Cattlin (tl); WildPictures (cr); Premaphotos (b). **38 Getty Images:** Tim Melling. **39 Dreamstime.com:** Dwphotos.
41 Dreamstime.com: Fesus Robert (crb); fotoknips (cla); Pitchayarat2514 (ca); Gordan Jankulov (cra). **42 Alamy Images:** Nature Collection (clb, crb).
Dreamstime.com: Photomyeye (cla). **44 123RF.com:** Martin Deja (tc, ftr).
Jacket images: _Front:_ Corbis: Patrick Pleul / dpa; **Dorling Kindersley:** Jacinto Valter ca, cra; **FLPA:** ImageBroker tc;
Fotolia: Norman Pogson cla; _Back:_ **Alamy Images:** Nature Collection bc; **Dreamstime.com:** Tharvron Posri tl
All other images © Dorling Kindersley
For further information see: www.dkimages.com

A WORLD OF IDEAS:
SEE ALL THERE IS TO KNOW
www.dk.com

Contents

Our Bee Friends

Bees are amazing! They help flowers make fruits and seeds. They give us sweet **honey**. So let's find out what makes a bee so special.

Chapter 1

What is a Bee?

A bee is an insect.
Like all insects, it has
six legs. It has a body
made up of three parts.

It has two pairs of wings.
Buzz, buzz, buzz!
A bumblebee beats its
wings so fast it makes
a buzzing sound.

Close-up View

Let's **ZOOM** in close.

A bee has
a hairy body
and face.

It has two
big eyes
and three
little ones.

It has a
very, very
long tongue.

On its legs, there
are little baskets
to collect
yellow **pollen**.

All these features
help a bee do its job.

From Egg to Bee

A bee starts life as a tiny egg inside a **wax cell**. A white grub called a **larva** hatches from the egg. Now the larva must eat and eat and eat…

egg

larva

bee

and grow fatter and fatter
until it turns into a **pupa**.
It sleeps for a long time.
When it wakes up,
an adult bee flies out.

AMAZING Bee Facts

Bee math

Honeybees build **honeycombs** with perfect six-sided cells.

Busy bees

Bees must visit two million flowers to make one jar of honey.

Sweet story

A worker bee
makes about
one-twelfth of
a teaspoon
of honey
in its lifetime.

Ouch!

A bee will
only sting
if you disturb it,
and only
female bees
have a **stinger**.

Chapter 2

Bees and Flowers

A bee is a flower's best friend. It helps the flower make seeds to make more flowers. It also helps the flower make the fruits and crops we eat.

The flower has food for
the bee—sugary **nectar**
and powdery pollen.

Sweet Nectar

A bee smells the flower and flies to it. It lands on a petal looking for the sweet, sugary juice.

The bee uncurls its long tongue and dips it deep inside the flower. **Sip, sip, sip!** It sucks up the nectar.

Petal Signposts

Bees see colors differently from you and me. They can see blues and purples, yellows and oranges. These are usually their favorite colors.

They can also see extra colors with their eyes. Sometimes the petals have markings that only a bee can see. These are like signposts for bees—this way for a sweet treat!

A bee sees the yellow flower like this.

Spreading Pollen

A bee may visit more than 50 flowers during one trip. As the bee flies from flower to flower, pollen sticks to its hairy body.

The bee combs some of the pollen into the baskets on its legs. Some of the pollen sticks to the bee's hairy body. When the bee flies to other flowers, this pollen brushes off.

Bee Dancing

Bees are great dancers. They dance to tell other bees the news.

Round dance

A bee dances in a circle.

This means there is food close by.

Waggle dance

A bee dances
in a figure 8 shape.

There is a **waggle**
in the middle.

It tells the other bees
the way to the nectar.

Chapter 3

Bee Families

The honeybee lives in a big family group. Each bee has its own special job to do. Beekeepers provide a home for the bees called a beehive. They can keep their bees safe and collect the honey.

Beekeepers always leave enough honey for the bees to eat.

Who's Who in the Hive

The biggest bee of all is the mother bee, called the Queen. Her job is to lay eggs. Next in size are the drones, the male bees. All the rest of the bees are females, called the worker bees.

Busy Bees

The worker bees are busy all day. Some look after the baby bees (larvae). They make a special food called royal jelly for the larvae. Some look after the Queen, feeding her royal jelly and grooming her.

Other workers guard
the nest, keep it clean, and
build new cells. While others
fly out of the hive to find
nectar and pollen.

Wild Bees

Wild honeybees can build their nests in a hollow tree, in a cave, or under a roof. They build a nest with wax cells. They make honey and store it for the winter. There are now a fewer number of bees in the wild. This is sad news.

All About
HONEY

Honey is the only food made by insects that we can eat.

When a bee brings nectar back to the nest, it passes the nectar to another bee.

This bee chews and chews the nectar and turns it into honey.

The bees store the honey in wax cells that make up a honeycomb.

Chapter 4

Bee Spotting

Not all bees live in big
groups like the honeybee.
Some bees live alone and
build their own special nests.

Some bees build their
nests in a crack in a wall
or a hole in the ground.
They lay their eggs and
leave them to hatch.

Builder Bees

Some bees build unusual nests.

If you see a
mound of soil
on the grass,
it could be the
door to the nest
of a lawn bee.

A carpenter bee
chews a hole in
wood to make
its nest.

Look out for neat round holes in a leaf. A leafcutter bee may have made them.

It builds a nest like a tube out of leaves and cuts a circle for a lid.

Garden Bees

One of the first bees you will see in spring is the bumblebee. They are hairy and striped, and are bigger than honeybees.

Bumblebees live in small family groups. They live in nests in the ground or in piles of dead leaves.

Be a Friend to Bees

Bees are very important in helping plants make the food we eat. We can help bees by planting flowers in a pot or a window box. Why not leave a patch for wild flowers to grow in a garden at home or at school?

Bees like flowers with lots of nectar and pollen. Here are some of them:

bluebell   hollyhock   clover

daisy   lavender

Perhaps your school could have a beehive. Then you can all eat lots of honey!

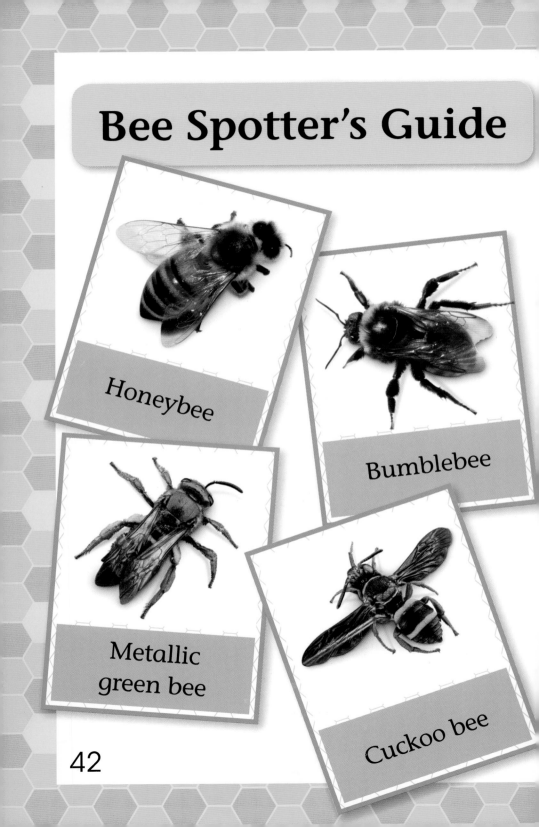

Bee Spotter's Guide

Honeybee

Bumblebee

Metallic green bee

Cuckoo bee

Amazing Bees Quiz

1. How many parts make up
   a bee's body?

2. Who is the biggest bee
   in a beehive?

3. Which is the only food made by
   insects that we can eat?

4. What sticks to a bee's body
   as it hunts for nectar?

5. What are female bees
   also called?

Answers on page 45.

Glossary

honey thick, sweet syrup made by bees

honeycomb group of wax cells where bees live and store honey

larva newly hatched wingless grub that will become an insect

nectar sweet liquid found in flowers used to make honey

pollen fine powder found on flowers

pupa larva changing into an adult insect

44

stinger sharp, needlelike part of a bee's body

waggle short, quick movement up and down or from side to side

wax cells perfect six-sided holes that make up a honeycomb

Answers to the Amazing Bees Quiz:
1. Three; **2**. Queen bee; **3**. Honey;
4. Pollen; **5**. Worker bees.

45

Guide for Parents

DK Readers is a four-level interactive reading adventure series for children, developing the habit of reading widely for both pleasure and information. These books have an exciting main narrative interspersed with a range of reading genres to suit your child's reading ability. Each book is designed to develop your child's reading skills, fluency, grammar awareness, and comprehension in order to build confidence and engagement when reading.

Ready for a *Beginning to Read* book

YOUR CHILD SHOULD

- be familiar with using beginning letter sounds and context clues to figure out unfamiliar words.
- be aware of the need for a slight pause at commas and a longer one at periods.
- alter his/her expression for questions and exclamations.

A VALUABLE AND SHARED READING EXPERIENCE

For many children, reading requires much effort, but adult participation can make this both fun and easier. So here are a few tips on how to use this book with your child.

TIP 1 Check out the contents together before your child begins:

- read the text about the book on the back cover.
- flip through the book and and stop to chat about the contents page together to heighten your child's interest and expectation.
- make use of unfamiliar or difficult words on the page in a brief discussion.
- chat about the nonfiction reading features used in the book, such as headings, captions, recipes, lists, or charts.

TIP 2 Support your child as he/she reads the story pages:

- give the book to your child to read and turn the pages.

- where necessary, encourage your child to break a word into syllables, sound out each one, and then flow the syllables together. Ask him/her to reread the sentence to check the meaning.

- when there's a question mark or an exclamation point, encourage your child to vary his/her voice as he/she reads the sentence. Demonstrate how to do this if it is helpful.

TIP 3 Chat at the end of each page:

- the factual pages tend to be more difficult than the story pages, and are designed to be shared with your child.

- ask questions about the text and the meaning of the words used. These help to develop comprehension skills and awareness of the language used.

A FEW ADDITIONAL TIPS

- Always encourage your child to try reading difficult words by themselves. Praise any self-corrections, for example, "I like the way you sounded out that word and then changed the way you said it, to make sense."

- Try to read together everyday. Reading little and often is best. These books are divided into manageable chapters for one reading session. However, after 10 minutes, only keep going if your child wants to read on.

- Read other books of different types to your child just for enjoyment and information.

Series consultant, **Dr. Linda Gambrell**, Distinguished Professor of Education at Clemson University, has served as President of the National Reading Conference, the College Reading Association, and the International Reading Association.

Index

AUG   2016